Turning Tragedy into Hope

*Becoming the Person You Never
Even Imagined You Could Be*

CINDY CURTIS JOHNSON

Endorsements

"Death of a child is an emotional roller coaster, no matter what the cause. This book is an excellent source for the grieving process, coping, and turning tragedy into triumph."

Keri Bunasky, BA/Social Worker

"Loved, loved, loved the book. Cried a lot but it was great. Brandon's life, cut far too short, should be an opportunity for us to realize that we should count our blessings… no matter what form they come in."

Sonya Smith Ellis

Turning Tragedy into Hope

*Becoming the Person You Never
Even Imagined You Could Be*

CINDY CURTIS JOHNSON

CROSSBOOKS

CrossBooks™
A Division of LifeWay
1663 Liberty Drive
Bloomington, IN 47403
www.crossbooks.com
Phone: 1-866-879-0502

© 2011 Cindy Curtis Johnson. All rights reserved.

No part of this book may be reproduced, stored in a retrieval system, or transmitted by any means without the written permission of the author.

First published by CrossBooks 12/6/2011

ISBN: 978-1-4627-1207-6 (sc)
ISBN: 978-1-4627-1209-0 (hc)
ISBN: 978-1-4627-1208-3 (e)

Library of Congress Control Number: 2011961470

Printed in the United States of America

This book is printed on acid-free paper.

Any people depicted in stock imagery provided by Thinkstock are models, and such images are being used for illustrative purposes only.

Certain stock imagery © Thinkstock.

Because of the dynamic nature of the Internet, any web addresses or links contained in this book may have changed since publication and may no longer be valid. The views expressed in this work are solely those of the author and do not necessarily reflect the views of the publisher, and the publisher hereby disclaims any responsibility for them.

Special thanks to:

My son, Brandon, whose suicide inspired me to begin living the life I never had the courage to live before. I will miss you until our reunion in heaven and will love you forever!

My daughter, Krissie, who has shown me how much a person can truly love another from the moment of conception and who has a passion for life I can only aspire to attain. I love you so much and am so truly proud and blessed to be your mother.

My soon-to-be son-in-law, Daniel, who has a heart for helping others and has encouraged me and my daughter every day since Brandon's death to grieve and heal at our own pace and in our own way. I love you and am so glad you are going to be a part of our family. Thank you for loving Krissie and Noah and for being there for us all during the most difficult time of our lives.

My grandson, Noah, who is the true "love of my life." Your smile and laughter are what keep me going on my darkest days. I thank God *every day* for you.

My husband, Glenn. Your presence in my life has shown me how strong a person I really am. Thank you for loving me, Krissie, Brandon, and Noah.

My parents, for your love and support and for bringing me up in a Bible-based Southern church.

My friends, for not only being there for me when this tragedy occurred but for also encouraging me to follow my dreams even when they didn't always make sense.

This book is dedicated to everyone who has experienced difficult times and/or unimaginable tragedy and now wants to make a true difference by becoming a new and better you.

Contents

Foreword ix
Glenda Warren, MBA

Introduction. xi

Chapter 1: Identify All Your Tragedies 1

Chapter 2: Allow Yourself to Feel Whatever You Feel. 23

Chapter 3: Learning from Life's Difficulties and Tragedies 47

Chapter 4: Identifying the Person You Were and Wanted to Be . . . 67

Chapter 5: Identifying the Person You Want to Become. 85

Chapter 6: Forgiving and Letting Go of Past Hurts 95

Chapter 7: Hope for a Bright and Productive Future 101

Foreword

Glenda Warren, MBA

For the past ten years, Cindy Johnson has been a part of my life. I remember the first time that we met years ago. Cindy was a marketing director for the Home Health Agency, and I worked for a local nursing home. Cindy impressed me with her great energy, smile, and enthusiasm. Cindy is such a special person, with a warm spirit and kind heart, that I am truly honored to have her in my life. Therefore, you can only imagine my joy when Cindy asked me to read her book. It was such a privilege and an honor that I considered to be a blessing.

Finally, a book that is refreshing to the soul, a joy to the spirit, and a natural way of healing. This book allows an individual to search the depths of his or her essence by acknowledging his or her inner pain, struggles, and regrets; however, through it all, Cindy gives us a holistic approach to finding where we should be. She provides insights for the audience to face their storms, with a spiritual approach to move forward in bliss.

I would recommend that everyone read this book. It does not stereotype, label, or categorize. It is for anyone that has experienced a tragedy or had pain. Cindy Johnson and her family experienced an unimaginable loss, but through it all, Cindy has shown a courage and bravery that can only be learned through this book.

Introduction

As mentioned in the dedication, this book is being written for everyone who has ever experienced difficult times and/or a tragedy. At one point or another in life, most of us will have to endure something so painful that we couldn't have ever believed we would be able to survive it—certainly not imagined we could become stronger from the experience.

First, let me say that I am not an expert on this subject. What I am writing is from my own personal experience. I have a bachelor's degree in social work. I am not a doctor, nor do I have any type of advanced degree. Although I have read a lot about grief, loss, and self-help, what I am writing in this book comes directly from my *heart* and my own personal experiences and journeys.

On September 11, 2009, my husband and I received that knock on the door all parents fear but few think will ever happen. At 3:12 AM, we were handed a note from the Clarksville police telling us to contact the hospital ER in Murfreesboro, Tennessee, because something had happened to our son. At that time, Brandon was beginning his third year at MTSU. I had talked to him on the phone mere hours before this knock. When we finally got through to a person willing to talk to us, we were told that our son had "shot himself in the head and had died as a result of a self-inflicted gunshot wound." I felt as if not only had my son's life ended that day, but mine as well. Actually, I was correct. Life as I knew it did die with Brandon. At that very moment and for months to come, I felt like I was being punished. I thought my life was worse than anyone else's. I truly went into a dark place where I felt sorry for myself and wasn't willing or able to see all my blessings that still existed and continued to be there in spite of this horrific loss.

My life certainly hasn't been an easy one, but as I share my story with others, I find out how truly fortunate and blessed my life has been. Until September 11, 2009, I really was more blessed than I recognized. I think most of us take good times for granted until something happens that changes our life as we knew it before. I had definitely experienced some difficult times prior to Brandon's death, but nothing hurt as badly or changed my life as much. Absolutely nothing could have prepared me for Brandon's suicide. Without a doubt, this was and is the most painful event of my life. There have been days I really didn't want to continue living. On many different occasions, I would have preferred to remain in a dark room under the covers and *never* come out. There have been days when I thought Brandon was the smart one for ending it all.

I certainly could have allowed this tragedy to consume me. My life as I knew it prior to my son's suicide definitely ended the same day he died. I could have chosen to simply exist, but I choose to live. Really *live!*

It is no longer good enough for me to simply go through life one day at a time without a true purpose. I want to make a difference in the lives of others in ways I never believed or even imagined I could before Brandon's death. I want to inspire others who have suffered from tragedy to redirect their pain and turn it into hope for a bright and productive future.

Chapter 1

Identify All Your Tragedies

Woe is me because of my hurt! My wound is grievous; but I said, Truly this is my grief, and I must bear it.
—Jeremiah 10:19

First, it is important for everyone to realize that what one person considers an unimaginable tragedy, another person may not. Some of the definitions Merriam-Webster lists for tragedy are: 2a: a disastrous event: calamity b:misfortune. I've always been told what a strong person I am. I certainly can't take the credit for that. From a very early age, I formed a strong relationship with God. I have always leaned on him and his word in times of trials and tragedies in my life. He has given me more strength than I ever imagined was possible.

Through the worst tragedy in my life, the suicide of my son Brandon, my entire perception of tragedy has changed. What I used to view as tragedies, I now realize, for me, were just minor setbacks. I really want to be clear here: I am not one to judge. If you haven't experienced a loss as devastating as the death of a child, that doesn't mean what you have experienced isn't an unimaginable tragedy to you. You must identify everything you see as a tragedy or loss in your life and deal with it before you can move on and become the person you never even imagined you could be.

Hopefully you've been fortunate enough in this life to have experienced life's ups and downs with very little unimaginable tragedy. Maybe you have experienced what you considered to be one or two unimaginable tragedies. I, fortunately, think I have experienced one true tragedy. If you had asked me prior to my son's death, my answer would certainly have been different.

As I share my story of loss, I find more and more people who have experienced multiple tragedies. Some have shared with me that they lost a grandfather as a result of suicide when they were young children and then, years later, lost a brother to suicide. Others have shared their stories of losing two or more family members as a result of suicide.

I have also witnessed the joy of pregnancy with more than one of my co-workers, only to have the birth be an incredibly heartbreaking experience. The children were born looking like perfect little angels, but without heartbeats.

I have a childhood friend whose mother was diagnosed with cancer when we were teenagers, and later died as a result of that cancer. On July 25, 1983, her father experienced a fall. He died six days later. On April 2, 1988, her brother, a doctor, was driving home from work. He was in a car accident and died instantly. This same friend went through a very messy divorce after learning her ex-husband had molested one of their daughters and had been extremely abusive toward her son.

Another childhood friend of mine lost her husband, the love of her life, in a farming accident. Then years later, their youngest son, at six years old, was diagnosed with terminal cancer and died at the age of seven.

Days after my twenty-year high school class reunion, the star running back from our 1982 championship football team was killed in a head-on collision. He left a wife and two young boys.

I encourage you stop reading at this point and write down everything that you consider to be tragedies in your life. Elaborate on them. Put into writing your reason for believing they are tragedies. I am going to do the same. Later in this book, we will refer back to our lists and see how we can turn each and every one of them into *hope* for the future!

Things You Considered Tragedies in the Past

___
___
___
___
___
___
___
___
___
___
___
___
___
___
___
___
___
___
___
___

Things You Considered Tragedies in the Past

Things You Considered Tragedies in the Past

Things You Considered Tragedies in the Past

Things You Considered Tragedies in the Past

Things I Considered Tragedies in My Life
Prior to Brandon's Suicide

1. Being an only child
2. My father's hospitalization
3. The death of my grandfather
4. My friend's alcoholism
5. The suicide of a close friend
6. My divorce
7. The death of my best friend's father
8. The death of my friend's seven-year-old son
9. The death of my ex-mother-in-law

I think it is important that we allow ourselves to feel whatever we feel about every situation we see as tragedies that affect us. That is why I am going to elaborate on the list above and explain why I felt these things were tragedies for me.

1. **<u>Being an only child</u>**
   Growing up, I was so envious of my cousins, mother, and friends who had siblings. There were so many times I wished and prayed for a brother or sister. I had several very close friends, but it just wasn't the same as having someone blood-related to me who shared both parents. This loneliness led to my determination to have two children despite health risks. When I had a very difficult pregnancy with my daughter, I was determined to have another child so my daughter never had to feel the loneliness I felt. How ironic is it that some of the first words out of my daughter's mouth when I told her that her brother had taken his own life were, "Now who will be here to help me take care of you and Dad when you are old? Brandon was supposed to be here!"

You are probably thinking being an only child is certainly not a tragedy! I, of course, realize that now. When I was growing up, however, I did believe it was tragic that I didn't have a brother or sister to share my life experiences with. It took me until middle school to really feel comfortable around others. I was a very shy, quiet, introverted child. I didn't feel like I fit in with other children because most of them had siblings. As a matter of fact, as I look back on it, the first best friends I made in school were, like me, only children.

2. **My father's hospitalization**

I will never forget how hopeless I felt when my dad had to be hospitalized due to anxiety. I didn't understand *why* God would allow such a thing to happen. In my mind, my dad was a good man. He went to church, and he had a very hard life growing up. He, like me, didn't have any brothers or sisters. He didn't have the support system my mother and other people who have siblings had. My mother, his mother, and I were all he had. His dad died when he was three years old. His mother loved him, but she didn't really show love the way most people do. She was not very affectionate, and he, in my opinion, had raised himself and her, rather than her raising and taking care of him.

My father's hospitalization was compounded by the fact that no one wanted to talk about it. They still don't, to this very day.

I remember going to visit him at the hospital. He refused to see me. I didn't understand at the time. He always gave my mother something he had made me. I specifically remember a belt that had my name and a belt buckle on it. I was going through a stage where I loved wearing cowboy boots and a cowboy hat, so the belt was a perfect gift. I prized it like nothing I had ever received before. Actually, to be honest, it is probably still my most prized gift ever because I don't really remember my dad giving me anything before that, certainly not something he made especially for me.

I had accepted Jesus as my Lord and Savior prior to my dad's hospitalization, but I certainly began to question my spiritual faith during this time.

I have to confess to you all, this is the first time I have ever written about my father's psychiatric hospitalization. I recognize, after writing this, this event in my life influenced me by making me want to help others. I chose to enter the mental health field as a result of this single event.

I started writing case studies and acting out plays where I was the psychiatrist. I knew from the moment of his hospitalization that I was meant to help others. It was several years later when I chose social work as a profession. I actually had a teacher and cheerleading sponsor who was a social worker. She was my favorite teacher of all time, and she inspired me to become a social worker simply because I wanted to be like her. One of the things she did for our cheerleading squad was write a quote about each of us. I will never forget what she wrote about me. She said, "To Cindy, the one with the smallest body and biggest heart, I give respect to the one who always gives her all!" Those words have stuck with me all these years and meant so much to me! Her influence and belief in me helped create the person I am today. I am eternally grateful to her.

3. **The death of my grandfather**
I always idolized my grandfather. In my eyes, he was the perfect man. He was strong, handsome, and loving. I knew no matter

what mistakes I made, he would always take my side and be one of my biggest supporters. He was my hero.

I spent a lot of time with my grandparents growing up. They ran a little country store behind their house. Because my mother and father worked, I would ride the bus to my grandparents' house and stay with them until my mother got off work and came to pick me up.

My grandfather was an avid fisherman. I just loved going fishing with him. Some of my fondest memories growing up were of going to my great-aunt and uncle's farm with my grandfather and cousin and fishing from the banks.

My grandfather had an offbeat sense of humor. He loved the fact, as did I, that I wasn't afraid to dig up worms and bait my own hook, while my male cousin didn't like to touch or bait his hook.

My grandfather loved to play cards (rook in particular). He was a very poor loser and an even worse winner. He didn't like for many people to be his partners; however, he always showed patience with me and usually chose me to be his partner.

At sixty-nine years of age, my grandfather was diagnosed with an aortic aneurysm. He had emergency surgery and, according to his doctors, died on the operating table three times. Despite all he experienced, he made it through the surgery and lived another ten years. He was here for the births of both of my babies and even saw me happily married to my current husband.

At seventy-nine years of age, my grandfather had not been feeling well. He went to the hospital for a routine arteriogram and died on the table. Because he was hooked up to life support for the procedure and didn't have a living will, he was kept alive on machines for three weeks. He never regained consciousness. On June 21, 1992, which just happened to be Father's Day, he was taken off life support and died.

Although I am incredibly grateful for the times I had with him, I still miss him every day of my life. Until the death of my son, nothing else had ever hurt as much as the death of my grandfather.

4. **My friend's alcoholism**

My best friend since elementary school has always been a person who loved to live life on the edge. She and I began experimenting with alcohol and drugs at an early age. The difference is, I stopped. Until recently, she did not.

I've been fortunate in that I have never had an addictive personality. I started smoking cigarettes when I was in middle school. For years, I smoked at least a pack a day. When I found out I was pregnant with my first child, I stopped smoking that day. I just put the cigarettes down and didn't smoke again until I had stopped breastfeeding her. I started smoking in between pregnancies and again, as soon as I found out I was pregnant with my second child, stopped smoking. I didn't start smoking again until I went through my divorce. As soon as my current husband explained to me that he didn't want to lose me as a result of lung cancer due to smoking, I stopped and haven't smoked in over nineteen years.

Drinking alcohol was a true problem for me when I was in college. I never have liked the taste of it. I drank alcohol in an attempt to escape reality. I drank to "get drunk." God truly looked out for me. There were many nights I drove after drinking. I easily could have killed myself or, worse yet, someone else.

Unfortunately, for my best friend, addiction continues to be an issue. Miraculously, during the first few days after Brandon's suicide, she was like her "former self," before the alcoholism took hold of her and changed her. She was totally and completely there for me. I know God gave her that strength and allowed her to be the person I needed to lean on during those first days.

I view her addiction as a tragedy for me because it took her from me for years. There have been many times when I longed for my sober friend. Even now, she is always one drink from relapse. She calls me when she's in crisis and needs my help. The majority of times when I have called her over the past few years, she has been impaired to the point where she couldn't even carry on a normal conversation. I have missed my friend so much. Many times, it has felt like the person I know her to be has died, even though she is still here on earth. Addiction is such a sad thing to witness.

5. **The suicide of a close friend**

I had a friend who suffered from depression and suicidal thoughts for years. He was one of the kindest people I have ever known. If you didn't know him well, you would have thought he was one of the happiest people alive. He had a terrific sense of humor and an incredible gift of making others around him laugh. He truly was the kind of person who would give someone the shirt off his back if they needed it.

Prior to his completed suicide, he had attempted many times. He obviously suffered from depression. He also had an addictive personality. He drank large amounts of alcohol and experimented with legal and illegal drugs.

When my friend took his own life, he had been diagnosed with cancer and was in a lot of pain. His wife had filed for divorce. Unlike previous attempts, this time, he didn't call anyone to tell them how he was feeling.

Although I always considered him a friend, he was far closer to my best friend and my cousin. My cousin actually spoke at his funeral. My best friend wept in her seat as her mother and husband comforted her.

For me, his death was a tragedy for us all. He had the voice of an angel and one of the kindest hearts I have ever witnessed. I continue to think of him often, especially since Brandon died by suicide, too.

6. **<u>My divorce</u>**

When I got married at twenty years of age, I truly took my wedding vows seriously. I intended to stay married to the same person for my entire life. I knew I didn't have the feelings for my husband that I had for my first "true love." I just thought there were different kinds of love.

My marriage was rocky from the start. We were both so young. I think we loved each other as much as we were capable of at that point and time in our lives. I will never regret our marriage because without it, I wouldn't have had my children.

We stayed together for seven years, were married for five years, and had two children together, but we fought a lot. I absolutely believe I would have stayed in that unhealthy relationship until the day I died had it not been for my wanting better for my children.

I will never forget how sad I was when I moved out of the house my husband and I had purchased together and back in with my parents. I had no job, no car, and no money. I literally left with my children and the clothes on our backs. It was such a scary time.

Within days, I had a job and had begun a new life. It was difficult, and I certainly considered it a tragedy. I never like to fail at anything, and I felt like a failure for not being able to make my marriage work. I believed that I had let my children down by not being able to make things work with their biological father. I felt like I had let God down because I did not honor my wedding vows.

7. **The death of my best friend's father**

I know there are things in life that we just aren't meant or equipped to understand. My best friend's father's death certainly seemed to fall into that category. He had recently retired. He only received one social security check before his death. He was one of those people who didn't like to go to doctors. I think he probably knew something was wrong, but he chose to ignore the warning signs and refused to go to the doctor.

I'll never forget my father calling to tell me that one of his neighbors had found him out in his garden dead. I will always remember the pain in the eyes of my best friend and her family when I first saw them just minutes after they had been told of his death. Why, when he was finally ready to enjoy retirement, was his life so suddenly, without warning, ended?

I viewed this as a tragedy in my life because he was like a second father to me. While growing up, I had stayed at their house almost as much as I had at my own. I had spent a lot of time with him. I felt cheated. I felt so sorry for his family. I felt especially sorry for his wife, who never got to enjoy spending their retirement years together, and for his new grandchild, who would never have her grandfather here to see her grow up.

8. **The death of my friend's seven-year-old**
   Mere months prior to my son's death was the devastating news that the little son of one of my high school friends had been diagnosed with brain cancer. I couldn't believe it. What more was my friend going to have to endure?

You may remember that earlier in the book, I mentioned having a friend who lost her husband in a farming accident and then lost a son to cancer. This is that friend.

This friend has a faith in God I can only aspire to have. She goes on mission trips, she is a nurse, she is very active in her church, and she is just one of those truly "good people."

She and her first husband were so good together. When you saw them, you could just see the love they shared for each other. They had three beautiful children together. Her little boy, diagnosed with cancer, was their youngest child.

For nine months, I read my friend's daily accounts of her child's struggle via Caring Bridge. There were good days and bad days but always *hope!* There were so many people praying for this little boy. I just knew he was going to be healed. I couldn't imagine God allowing my friend and her family to endure such pain again. Wasn't the death of her husband *enough?* Obviously, it was *not!*

My friend's little boy showed strength and courage throughout his journey. He even said that he was ready to go and be with his daddy and God in heaven.

I viewed my friend's son's death as a tragedy in my life because it absolutely consumed my thoughts daily. It forced me to realize that life is precious and can change in the blink of an eye. I couldn't imagine anything worse than losing a child. I couldn't fathom sitting, watching my child suffer, and not being able to do anything to help him.

9. **The death of my ex-mother-in-law**
I'm certain of one thing in this life, and that is that there will never be another person like my ex-mother-in-law. She had the ability to make me laugh when I didn't think anyone could do it. You know how sometimes in life, you just meet those people you know you were destined to know? She was that person to me. For years, she was my sounding board. She was there when I needed her most, though never in person. She just couldn't seem to get it together enough to be there in person for anyone. She was just always there by phone, and we seemed, from the very first meeting, to be in tune with each other. Without fail, I would get a phone call from her when I needed it most. She always seemed to be able to tell when I was having a bad day. She would call and say, "What's wrong? I can hear it in your voice!"

I'm not sure I ever felt the way I should have about her son, but one thing is certain: there has never been a day that I haven't felt truly blessed to have known her. I am sure I am a better person for having had her in my life.

No matter what was going on in my life, whether it was when I was still married to her son or after we divorced, I always knew I could call her and she would be there. She just listened. She would offer advice only if I asked for it. She never got upset if I didn't take her advice. She was just always there to listen. We all really need someone like that in our lives.

What's ironic about this is that her children, grandchildren, and ex-husband didn't see the same qualities in her that I saw. She was an extremely disorganized person. She wasn't there for her children or grandchildren in the ways they needed her to be. For me, she was there just the way I needed her. That's not to say that she didn't "let me down" too at times. She did. She was human, after all. I guess I just accepted her the way she accepted me, and I didn't expect more of her than she was able to give.

Her death was such a tragedy in my life. I hadn't spoken to her for several months. That was normal for us. I think we just assumed we would be there for each other whenever we needed. I received a phone call from one of her best friends telling me she was in the hospital in congestive heart failure. I'll never forget it because it was late in the day and she had been hospitalized many times during the past few years of her life. I made the decision to wait until the next day to call her. My thinking was that she would still be there because this wasn't anything new for her. When I called her room the following morning, I was told that she was in ICU in a coma. I never got to hear her voice again or to say good-bye to her.

I have experienced some major things in my life since her death. When I had my hysterectomy in 2008, I wanted to call her and talk to her about it. I remembered our conversations about her hysterectomy and feelings related to it. I was certain she was the only person who would have understood how I felt.

When the police came to our door and we found out Brandon had taken his own life, I wanted to call her. I knew she wouldn't judge his act, or me. I knew if she were still alive, she would be able to comfort me in a way no one else could. She, of course, wasn't there, and I felt so much grief and anger. I needed her. Why did God have to take her so young? Didn't he know I still needed her to be here?

As you can see from the list above, prior to my son's suicide, I took on other people's tragedies and called them my own.

I think it is important that we allow ourselves to feel whatever we feel about every situation we see as difficult times and/or tragedies that affect us. Without the experience of those difficult times and extreme pain, none of us would be at the point where we are now—ready **to begin the journey toward becoming a new and better person!**

Unimaginable Tragedy...

Brandon's grave site.

CHAPTER 2

Allow Yourself to Feel Whatever You Feel

God is our refuge and strength, a very present help in trouble.
—**Psalm 46:1**

I'll never forget that knock on the door and hearing that my son had taken his own life! I felt like my heart stopped at that very moment. I didn't believe it at first; to be honest, two years later, I still don't believe it sometimes. When the police handed the note to my husband and me, I was convinced they had the wrong person. My son wouldn't, couldn't have taken his own life.

Six hours before his suicide, I had spoken to him on the phone. We had a wonderful conversation. He told me about the speech he had given that day. We talked about his nephew and how he was going to spoil him. He told me he was going to a friend's apartment to watch a football game, and we talked about him coming home the next weekend for a visit. He told me he loved me. I just knew he would not have taken his life—he would have known how much that would hurt his family. I told myself, even if he didn't care about anyone else, he would have thought of Noah and wouldn't have left his nephew.

Being a social worker, I knew the stages of grief. I must admit, I definitely was in shock and denial at first. I didn't believe the police when they said something had happened to Brandon Johnson. I just knew I would have felt something was wrong when we talked, or certainly my mother's intuition would have kicked in at the very moment his life ended. I hadn't felt that, so it had to be a mistake! They had to have the wrong person!

Even now, two years later, there are days when I have to allow myself to think Brandon is still in Murfreesboro; the reality is just too painful.

Don't let anyone tell you how you should feel or how long you should grieve. Grief is different for everyone. Tragedies make grief even more complicated. I remember people saying the first year would be the hardest. For me, that simply wasn't true. I felt numb for the first year. The second year was harder for me. That is when my anger, grief, and sadness really set in. I experienced times where I would get so angry at people. I still have those moments. Something as simple as seeing a mother and son in a photo, or at church, would make me so mad. I was mad that they didn't seem to appreciate that precious gift they were given, that that mother still had her son and I didn't. Then, I would feel guilt over the anger I felt. I tried to remind myself how blessed I was to have been chosen to be Brandon's mom for the twenty years he was on this earth. I would say to myself that we are all God's children and Brandon belonged to him, not me. Sometimes that helped me feel better, but sometimes it didn't help at all.

I believe it has been extremely important for me to identify all the stages of grief I have experienced. I think we all need to make a conscious effort to recognize and feel our pain! I'm not a person who likes to show weakness. I am a control freak! I know it! I recognize it! I admit it! I don't allow myself to cry in front of other people if I can help it at all. At Brandon's funeral, everyone kept telling me that it just hadn't hit me yet because I wasn't publicly crying. They were *wrong!* I saw my son in his casket. I knew he was dead. I just wasn't going to allow *anyone* to witness me falling apart! I prayed for the strength to make it through that day and God granted that to me. I have prayed every day since then for that same strength and God continues to grant it to me. Have I completely fallen apart in private? *Yes—many, many* times.

I have spoken about Brandon's suicide to large and small groups of people. I have shared my story with many others who have lost someone to suicide. Although emotional, I have yet to cry when speaking about him. I have cried the entire drive home after these speaking engagements but have not yet broken down in front of anyone. It is as if God takes over, dries my tears, and gives me the words.

Let's explore the stages of grief now. The stages I am including here are those we use in our Survivors of Suicide support group meetings. There are five stages, just as there are in the Kubler-Ross model.

I plan to discuss my feelings during each stage, and I encourage you to utilize the note pages inserted at the end of each stage and do the same. We have to work through the pain to get to the healing!

Shock and Denial

I was most definitely in shock when I was first told of my son's death. I am quite sure I would have been in shock no matter what the cause of death. The fact that he took a shotgun he had used to hunt with, stuck it in his mouth, and pulled the trigger, resulting in instant death, made the shock and denial for me even greater!

In those first few moments after being told, all I could think of was our conversation six hours prior to his death. I remember feeling like I was watching myself. It was as if I was out of my own body, watching someone else being given the worst news possible and simply going through the necessary motions.

The first thing I thought about was how I had to get to my daughter, Krissie, and be the one to tell her first about her brother's death. In this time and age of social media, I was so afraid she would find out from Facebook or MySpace before I reached her apartment. I really don't remember the drive across town in those early morning hours. I do, however, remember the shock and intense pain on my daughter's face and in her voice when I told her that her brother was dead.

I have thought many times about the method of death—suicide—Brandon chose. I can't wrap my mind around any of it, even now. It just doesn't make sense to me that a twenty-year-old with so much potential could let anything make him feel so hopeless that he would think taking his own life was his best option.

The denial, for me, lasted a lot longer than the initial shock. There are days (really, I guess it more like hours now) when I still am in denial. Sometimes I pretend Brandon is still alive and well in Murfreesboro. I try to convince myself that he is there working, going to school, visiting with friends, etc.

There were and are still a lot of questions surrounding my son's suicide. For months, we didn't know that he had left a suicide note. Brandon's roommate's accounts of the day and night leading up to his death varied greatly depending upon with whom he was speaking. The police were very resistant to sharing details regarding their investigation of his death.

At first, I blamed his roommate, I blamed the police, and I blamed myself and everyone who had contact with Brandon the night of his suicide. In my mind, Brandon just couldn't have taken his own life. I just knew my son would have left a note, that he would have explained why he was making such a choice; he would have told his family in that note that he loved us.

Shock and Denial

Shock and Denial

Fear and Anger

*I sought Jehovah, and he answered me,
and delivered me from all my fears.*
—Psalm 34:4

Within hours of Brandon's death, I allowed fear to take control of me. I immediately thought of all the people in my life who had suffered several tragedies. I was convinced that something was going to take Krissie and Noah from me. Poor Krissie—I know I must have driven her crazy, calling her, texting her, begging her not to go anywhere. I just wanted her and Noah with me so I knew they were safe. I was convinced that if they were out of my sight, something terrible was going to happen to them as well. I remember Krissie saying to me, "Mom, I promise I'll be careful. You don't have to worry. I would never kill myself like Brandon did." I don't think she understood. I didn't think she was going to deliberately hurt herself; I just felt like I was being punished and God was taking my children from me because I wasn't a good enough person.

My fear has gotten better than it was at first. I still struggle with the fear at times. I think I always will, to some degree. Some days are better than others. When tragedy strikes other friends of mine or on those days when Brandon is on my mind even more than usual, my fear seems to get worse.

As I briefly mentioned in the "Shock and Denial" section, at first I blamed everyone, including myself, for Brandon's death. I was angry. I still struggle with the anger. In those first months, I was really angry with everyone except Brandon. I was still denying that he had completed suicide. There was still a part of me that thought someone else had to have taken his life. Despite all the evidence to the contrary, I just wasn't willing or able to accept my son's suicide at first.

When I finally did accept that he and only he was responsible for and actually had taken his own life, I became *extremely* angry with him.

Many survivors of suicide (people who have lost a family member or close friend as a result of suicide) whom I have spoken with over the past two years have told me how angry they are with God. I must admit, there have been moments when I, too, have been angry with God. Those moments haven't been very frequent. My anger has been directed more at situations and at people who haven't been there for me during this time.

Of course, my family and friends were there those first few days after Brandon's death. I was still in shock and denial then. I really felt like I was watching someone else. I didn't feel like it was happening to me. I truly appreciate them all being here then, but where have they been since? I know people don't know what to say, but there have been days, especially after that first year, that I have felt all alone. I really needed my family and friends more the second year, and they just weren't there for me. I realize they probably just don't know what to say to me, but I am *angry* at them for not being here when I needed them the most.

Recently, my anger has manifested itself when Brandon's friends graduated from college, when some of his cousins and friends got married, and when a co-worker's son graduated from the concrete industry management program at MTSU and got a job in Saint Louis, Missouri.

Brandon was supposed to have graduated in May of 2011. His major was concrete industry management, and he had already talked about wanting to get a job in Saint Louis when he graduated. I was so angry—actually, *angry* is probably not the right word; it was more like I felt an incredible pain—when my co-worker shared her excitement and joy over her son graduating with his degree in concrete industry management and his new job in Saint Louis. I was angry at myself for feeling resentment and envy toward her. It certainly wasn't her fault that she was so proud of her son's accomplishments and was proud to share her excitement with her co-workers. Then I realized I wasn't angry at her or her son. I was angry at God. I still don't understand why God allowed me accept a job six months after Brandon's death and have a co-worker whose son was at the same school, majoring in the same subject, and graduating at the same time Brandon should have had he not taken his own life. I felt like it was some type of cruel joke being played on me.

I am *angry* that people judge me for the decision my son made.
I am *angry* that people judge my son for his decision.
I am *angry* that my son is no longer here.
I am *angry* that everyone else's lives continued to be the same, yet mine and my family's lives changed so dramatically the day Brandon died.
I am *angry* that people feel sorry for me.
I am *angry* that people treat me and my remaining family members differently now.

Don't get me wrong. I'm not angry every moment of every day. I have to be honest, though: the anger is still there, and the anger comes much more quickly to me now than it did prior to Brandon's suicide.

My mother recently told me that I need to let go of the anger and resentment I feel toward my extended family members and in-laws because it is only hurting me. Believe me, intellectually, I know that. I just haven't figured out a way yet to make that happen. I am praying daily for God to help me not to be angry or resentful. I wish I could say that I am anger- and resentment-free now, but I am not. It is still something I struggle with *every day!*

Fear and Anger

Fear and Anger

Guilt and Shame

*For the scripture saith, whosoever believeth
on him shall not be put to shame.*
—Romans 10:11

No matter how much I read or how many people tell me I'm not to blame for my son's decision, I still feel an incredible amount of guilt.

Brandon and I were extremely close when he was a little boy. He always wanted me to go on his school field trips, come to his classroom, and do everything with him. In 1997, he made the honor roll the entire school year. His father and I had told him he could go to Space Camp in Huntsville, Alabama, if he achieved this goal. When given the choice of which parent to take with him, Brandon chose me. I was so excited. We had such a terrific time there. It was wonderful and remains one of my fondest memories today.

When I overheard some of Brandon's classmates call him a "momma's boy," I became worried that he was going to be bullied and made fun of because of the close relationship we had. I began to encourage him to distance himself from me. At the time, I really believed I was doing what was in his best interest. Now I would give *anything* if I could have handled that situation differently. It should have been Brandon's decision, not mine. I blame myself every day for distancing myself from him. I fear that he thought I didn't love him as much because of it.

I also feel an incredible amount of guilt over not insisting that Brandon talk with a therapist when he was in high school. I was always worried that he was the type of person who was capable of completing suicide. He could be so happy one minute and so mad the next. I voiced my concerns to others, but they always said the same thing: "Don't think that way. He wouldn't do that." I blame myself for not listening to my own intuition.

I feel guilty over not picking up on his sadness during our last phone conversation. I have played our last conversation over and over in my head. I still can't figure out how I would have known anything was wrong. He seemed so happy. We had a great conversation. Despite the facts, I still feel guilty.

Shame has certainly accompanied my guilt and is something I've definitely experienced. Again, I think the fact that my son completed suicide has compounded this even further. There is still such a negative stigma attached to any type of mental illness. When people asked how he died, their faces change immediately when they are told it was a suicide.

Guilt and Shame

Guilt and Shame

Grief and Sadness

Mine eye wasteth away because of grief; It waxeth old because of all mine adversaries.
—**Psalm 6:7**

I imagine those of you reading this book have experienced grief and sadness at some point already in your lives. The grief and sadness I have experienced since my son's suicide are beyond my explanation. I will certainly attempt to explain it, but I'm certain words can't adequately describe the level of grief and sadness this tragedy has caused.

I had always heard people talk about unimaginable grief. I had certainly experienced grief and sadness prior to September 11, 2009. Even though I had had experiences that caused me to feel these emotions before, nothing ever could have prepared me for the level of grief and sadness which resulted from my son's suicide. There are days when I cry off and on all day long. I truly feel like my heart is broken. I miss him and long for him so much. I would give anything to see his smile, hear his voice, and hug him again.

Not only have I experienced the emotional pain, but I have also experienced physical pain. Sometimes the grief and sadness get so bad that I don't even want to get out of bed. I lost twenty pounds the first month after Brandon's death. I have experienced insomnia, anxiety, low blood pressure, low blood sugar, urinary tract infections, and depression.

Grief and sadness this great cause a person to change. I am not the same person I was before Brandon's death. What I have heard before from other people when they had a close family member die is true: a part of me died the day Brandon died. The person I was prior to that date doesn't exist anymore. I don't enjoy the things I enjoyed before. I used to love shopping, especially for clothes. Now material things just don't matter as much to me. That's not to say that I don't enjoy having nice things; I do. I just don't place the same amount of importance on them that I once did.

Grief and Sadness

Grief and Sadness

Acceptance and Hope

In the day that I called thou answeredst me, Thou didst encourage me with strength in my soul.
—Psalm 138:3

After two years, I believe I have accepted that my son is dead. That is not to say that I don't still have days where I tell myself otherwise just to make it through the day.

I accept that my son took his own life, and I no longer blame anyone, including him, for that. I have become an advocate for suicide awareness and prevention. I have learned so much, yet I still have so much more to learn.

After talking with his friends and other survivors of suicide, I believe Brandon was hurting. I know he drank with his friends at a party because his blood alcohol level was double the legal limit. I know he had a gun, got in a fight with his roommate, and made a permanent decision to address a temporary problem. I have come to realize that his decision had nothing to do with me or anyone other than Brandon. At that moment, he obviously viewed suicide as his only option. I don't believe he thought of anyone else or how they would feel. I believe he felt hopeless and helpless. I would give anything if he had made a different decision that night, but he didn't. I will miss him until we are reunited in heaven and will love him forever.

In order to move on with my life, I have to let go of Brandon. That's not to say I have to forget him or stop thinking of him. I just have to accept that he is gone from this Earth. I know a lot of people don't agree that he is in heaven. I do. I believe in a God who is full of love and kindness. I believe we are saved by Grace.

Brandon accepted Jesus as his Lord and Savior at a very early age. He was a loving and kind person. He made, in my opinion, a mistake when he took his own life. I do not believe he, in his right mind, would have done so. I believe God understood his pain and welcomed him to heaven. I believe he is in a better place, at peace, happy, and waiting to welcome his other family members and friends to heaven one day.

I now have *hope* for a bright future. I know that I am a better person for having had my son in my life for twenty years. I know that through this *tragedy,* I have become a better person. I know that if I can make it through the death of my son, I can make it through anything. I know that I have a purpose on this Earth that is greater than I ever imagined it could be, and I'm ready to start my journey to find the new and better me.

Acceptance and Hope

Acceptance and Hope

Chapter 3

Learning from Life's Difficulties and Tragedies

*It is good for me that I have been afflicted;
That I may learn thy statutes.*
—**Psalm 119:71**

I now look back on the things I used to consider tragedies in my life and realize that God was preparing me for the major tragedy I was going to later experience. It's amazing how God works in our lives. I truly believe he allowed me to witness tragedies in the lives of my friends so I would learn from them. I also believe he allowed certain difficulties in my life so I would be better prepared to face something I never imagined I would have the strength to face.

Let's now look back at those things we considered tragedies in our lives prior to our true *tragedies* and see how they helped prepare us for now! I encourage you to do the same thing with the list you compiled earlier.

Learning from Life's Difficulties and Tragedies

Learning from Life's Difficulties and Tragedies

Learning from Life's Difficulties and Tragedies

Learning from Life's Difficulties and Tragedies

Learning from Life's Difficulties and Tragedies

Learning from Life's Difficulties and Tragedies

1. **<u>Being an only child</u>**

   I absolutely hate it when people ask how many brothers and sisters I have! Without fail, when I respond that I am an only child, they say, "I bet you were spoiled rotten." I suppose this may have been true of some only children; however, it was simply not true for me. My parents tried really hard to make sure that I wasn't that "spoiled only child."

   Because I was an only child, I do believe I grew up faster than a lot of my peers. I can't totally attribute that to being an only child. It certainly was due to my personality, which, I am sure, was somewhat influenced by the fact that I was an only child.

   I have always been a strong-willed, opinionated person. My mother loves to tell stories about me correcting myself when I was barely able to talk. She has often told me about her hearing me in the kitchen getting into things she had told me to stay out of and saying, "Put that up. Put that back."

   I have always been a "take-charge" kind of person. It wasn't enough for me to be on a cheerleading squad; I had to be captain or co-captain. I like to be the person making the decisions. I am the leader, not the follower.

   Because I spent so much time with adults, I identified with them far more than with children my own age. Of course, I went through the rebellious teenage years, but even then, I had the voice of an adult in my head telling me that what I was doing was immature and *wrong!*

   I truly believe I am a stronger person because I am an only child. I haven't ever had siblings to lean on when times were tough.

I have always had to depend on myself and be comfortable spending time without anyone else around.

When I reflect on my feelings toward being an only child now, I realize it was a blessing, not a tragedy. It caused me to grow up feeling like I could handle anything. I just never imaged that "anything" would be the suicide of my son.

2. **<u>My father's hospitalization</u>**
   This event caused me to change more than any other event in my life until the suicide of my son. I immediately knew I wanted to help other people who needed help like my father. I was never ashamed that he had to be treated for anxiety. I didn't and still don't understand why there is such a negative stigma attached to any form of mental stress or illness. I admire people who are willing to seek help for any type of illness (especially mental health).

Without this event in my life, I'm certain I would not have become the person I am today. I became a social worker because I wanted to help others. When I was in college, I always thought I would want to work with children. When I found my first social work job, it was working with persons with developmental disabilities. I had residents ranging in age from ten to eighty years old. Even though I enjoyed working with the children, I found myself drawn to the older adults. Throughout my more-than-twenty-year career, I have found that I enjoy working the most with the senior population and particularly enjoy educating them and their caregivers on mental health issues.

As I stated previously, during my father's hospitalization, I questioned my faith. I questioned whether or not God existed. I was *angry* with God!

When Brandon died, I knew that God had been there for me many times after I doubted him and was angry with him when my father was hospitalized. I knew God would understand if I questioned him and was angry with him again. I think that is why I wasn't angry at God when everyone expected me to be. I knew it was he who helped me hold it together to plan Brandon's funeral, pick his gravesite, and handle all his affairs. I felt God's arms around me then, and I feel them *now!*

3. **The death of my grandfather**
I didn't realize how precious life was until my grandfather's death. He was so important to me.

I certainly knew that he would die at some point during my lifetime, but until his death, I never really allowed myself to imagine a day when he wouldn't be here. Even during those long three weeks when he was in the hospital on life support, I was still hoping for a miracle that would cause him to wake up and smile at me as if nothing had happened.

For years, I grieved for my grandfather. There are still times when I feel an overwhelming sense of sorrow over his death.

Brandon shared so many of my grandfather's qualities. He had his offbeat sense of humor, his temper, his love of fishing, and his "poor loser and even worse winner" traits. Some of Brandon's mannerisms, even though he didn't remember my grandfather, were the same, such as the way he would put his hands behind his neck and smile that crooked "I'm up to something" smile.

My grandfather had four children, seven grandchildren and two great-grandchildren before Brandon's birth, and yet Brandon was the first newborn baby my grandfather ever held. I will never forget the day when my grandfather picked up Brandon and laid him on his shoulder. They both looked so comfortable and at peace with each other. My grandfather and Brandon shared a bond that was undeniable. They are two of my favorite people *ever!*

I know that losing my grandfather helped prepare me for Brandon's death. I also know that my grandfather's unconditional love for me helped me become the person I am today.

4. **<u>My friend's alcoholism</u>**
   Seeing my best friend struggle with alcoholism has been a humbling experience for me. It has also made me feel incredibly grateful and blessed that I do not have the same problem. I could easily have become an alcoholic along with her. For years, we drank together. I thank God for allowing me to stop abusing alcohol and not become addicted.

   I do have some good news with regard to my friend. Recently, her family intervened, and she went to a treatment facility. It has been wonderful hearing her admit that she is an alcoholic. She still struggles daily but at least now admits her addiction and is on the road to recovery.

   I have missed my friend. I hate what alcohol has done to her. I must admit, I am angry about the fact that her addiction has kept us from the closeness we once shared.

   Without witnessing my friend's alcoholism, I don't think I would have been able to appreciate how truly blessed I am to not have such a daily struggle. As I've admitted already, I am a control freak. I can't imagine the torture I would feel if there was an addiction I was unable to control.

My friend, despite her alcoholism, has been there for me during the times I have needed her most. I know God put her in my life for more than a few reasons. She is like a sister to me. I love her dearly and look forward to her recovery.

5. **<u>The suicide of a close friend</u>**

    My friend's suicide was one of the most difficult things I have ever experienced. The fact that he had attempted suicide on many occasions and then actually completed it when everyone thought he was doing better made it extremely difficult to accept. I was raised to believe that suicide was an unforgivable sin. I was told that people who killed themselves went to hell instead of heaven. This was the first time I truly doubted that belief.

As I said earlier, my friend was so loving and kind. He could sing so beautifully. When people heard him sing, they often described his voice as that of an angel. I couldn't and still can't imagine him being anywhere but heaven. I just know he is singing with God and the angels.

When we were told of Brandon's suicide, I immediately thought of my friend. I remembered what the preacher said at his funeral about his belief that God is a loving God and that he believed my friend was in heaven. That comforted me so much.

I believe God put my friend in my life knowing that his suicide would help to prepare me for my son's. I wish my friend and Brandon had not done so. I wish they were both still here with us. I just know that God understands far more than I do. I know he has a plan for all of our lives. I thank God for the time I had with my friend and Brandon.

6. **<u>My divorce</u>**
    My divorce showed me that no matter how much I thought I could control my life, I couldn't. It showed me that people change and sometimes it is better to end a marriage than to remain in an unhappy one.

    When I went through my divorce, it forced me to grow up in ways I wouldn't have otherwise. All of a sudden, I was responsible solely for my and my children's financial and emotional well-being. I didn't have a house, a car, or money. I left with my children and the clothes on our backs. I had to move back in with my parents, get a job, and start my life all over. I quickly learned how strong I could be when I had to be. I no longer could count on my spouse's income or insurance benefits. It was up to me to provide for myself and my children.

    My first husband had convinced me that I couldn't survive on my own. I found out I could make it. Fortunately, I had family and friends that I could lean on, and I did just that. I worked hard and in six months was able to move into my own apartment and purchase furniture for it. With the help of my dad and my friend who completed suicide, I was able to purchase a used car, which I paid off early (two years before the loan was due in full).

    Without a doubt, my divorce helped me gain self-esteem and a sense of independence that I had lacked before. It caused me to look at myself in a different way. It forced me to hold myself accountable for my own and my children's well-being. It showed me that I could do it, with God's help, on my own!

    I have often heard people describe divorce as similar to death. It was the death of my marriage and the vows I planned to keep until the day I died. For me, though, it was more like a rebirth. I never wanted my children to grow up in a house with parents who fought and didn't show love toward each other.

The scared feelings I had when I left my first marriage were nothing compared to the feelings I had when Brandon died, but I know this experience helped prepare me.

7. **The death of my best friend's father**
My friend's father's death showed me how quickly your life can change. I remember his wife telling everyone about how she talked with him that morning before she left for work and then got the call that he was being taken to the hospital after being found lying face-down in his garden.

Her grief was so *great!* She and he had so many plans. They had a new granddaughter. He had just retired. They were supposed to be able to spend more time together and with their family. In an instant, all those hopes and dreams were gone.

I remember how incredibly sad I felt for his entire family. It didn't seem fair that he had worked so hard for all of those years and only received one social security check before dying. I was sad for me too because his death forced me to realize that life is way too precious to be taken for granted. I had always heard that but never really realized it until his death. One minute, he was working in his garden; the next, he was dead.

Witnessing the sadness and grief of my closest friend and her family most definitely helped to prepare me for Brandon's death. I have watched them, over the years, not forget him but move on with life. His wife has not remarried, as many people thought she would. She sold their house, moved to the town where her children and grandchildren live, bought an adorable condo, and made a new life for herself. I know her life isn't the way she had planned or hoped it would be. In spite of the death of her husband, she has continued to live.

I wish my friend's father had lived a longer life and been able to enjoy retirement. I wish his grandchildren had known him and been able to spend time with him. I wish my friend and her family hadn't had to experience such pain and sadness.

I believe everything in life happens for a reason. I know I am a better person for having known my friend's father. I'm grateful for the years he was here on earth with us. I'm grateful to God for allowing me to be there with his family during his funeral. I'm grateful that I was witness to their lives, although different without him, going on despite his death.

8. **The death of my friend's seven-year-old**
Of all the difficult times in my life, the death of my friend's seven-year-old son prepared me for my own *tragedy* more than any other event could have done. I still don't understand why she had to first endure the pain of his father's death and then his. I guess that is one of those things in life that are just not meant for us to understand.

My friend inspired me daily during her child's nine-month struggle with cancer. Her strength and continued devotion to God despite all the tragedies she had experienced made me want to be a better person. At that time, I really thought I could empathize with her. I actually prided myself on not simply sympathizing with others but being able to actually identify with them, put myself in their place, and feel what they were feeling. Of course, when Brandon died, I realized I wasn't able to do that before. I simply thought I could.

The pain felt at losing a child is so much greater than anything I had ever imagined. When my friend's little boy died, I thought about the people in my life who had died. I felt sorry for her and grieved for her with my past grief in mind. Since I had never experienced the death of a child, I had no idea of the pain my friend was experiencing.

I know God put my friend in my life for a reason. When Brandon died, I often thought of her daily posts where, no matter how bad a day her little boy was having, she was positive and giving praise to God. I admire her so much!

My friend continues to be such an inspiration to me. Her strength and ability to move on with her life and *really live* after two terrible tragedies give me *hope* for my future.

I am so proud to report that my friend is now remarried and is very happy. Her children are doing well, and they all have an extremely positive outlook on life. I know she still misses her first husband and youngest child every day, but she didn't allow the tragedies in her life to define her. She has moved on with life and continues to inspire others. I know that if she can do it with all of her tragedies, I certainly can as well.

9. **The death of my ex-mother-in-law**
I learned so much about who I wanted to and didn't want to be from knowing my ex-mother-in-law. She was one of those people who always talked about what she was going to do but just never got around to doing much, if any, of it. Her house was a disaster. She never threw away anything. She was one of

those people who would have you stop on the side of the road to pick up a rotten piece of wood. She always had *big* plans for everything.

I think one of the main reasons God brought my ex-mother-in-law into my life was because she was so different from anyone I had ever or have since met. She had a great sense of humor and loved to have fun, yet she often got really depressed and down. She experienced so many difficult times in her short lifetime. She got married before finishing high school and had two children with her first husband, who was abusive to her. They divorced and then remarried. They divorced a second time, and she married my ex-husband's father. She had the one child with him. Then she divorced him and married the love of her life. They weren't able to have children together, despite numerous pregnancies (all of which resulted in miscarriages). He cheated on her many times throughout their more-than-twenty-year marriage and eventually left her for a younger woman.

My ex-mother-in-law and I shared so much. We had phone conversations where we would talk for hours at a time. As I said earlier, she never judged me for anything. She simply listened, offered advice if I asked for it, and never got upset if I didn't accept her advice. I wish her children, her grandchildren, and the love of her life could have seen the qualities in her that I saw. I wish she could have loved them without having placed her expectations on them. It's unfortunate that her children and grandchildren felt that her love for them was contingent upon them doing what she wanted them to do. Sometimes, I think that if they had known all the trials she had experienced, they would have understood her better and would have been able to love her unconditionally.

It makes me incredibly sad that she died with her children not even speaking to her. They hadn't for years. She always hoped and longed for the day that her ex-husband would call to say that he had made a mistake when he left her and wanted her back. She swore she would tell him "no," but I knew how much she loved him and that she would have let him come back, no matter what.

My ex-mother-in-law made a lot of mistakes with her children, grandchildren, and ex-husbands. She often put others before her family, and her children, husband, and grandchildren, understandably, were hurt by that.

I remember every January 1, her New Year's resolution included making more time for my children. Without fail, that resolution was broken year after year. She always talked about clearing her house of all the clutter and had big dreams about becoming famous and having a lot of money. None of those things happened for her.

I learned so many things by knowing my ex-mother-in-law.

Some of those things include the following:

- Accept people for who they are, and don't try to change them.
- Never put off until tomorrow what you can do today.
- Always put your family first.
- Love unconditionally.
- Don't judge anyone else because you never know what they have experienced that has made them the way they are.
- Don't expect anyone else to make you happy; find your own happiness.

- Live every day as if it is your last.
- Appreciate all your blessings.

There is not a day that goes by that I don't think about my ex-mother-in-law and wish she was still here to make her dreams come true. I know she is in heaven. She just has to be.

Chapter 4

Identifying the Person You Were and Wanted to Be

Isn't it amazing how differently we are able to view those things we saw as tragedies or difficulties in our lives now that we have looked at them from a different point of view? Do you see how every event in our lives has helped to shape and make us into the people we are now?

I thought I was okay with the person I was before Brandon's death. Notice I say *okay*. I was never really happy with the person I had become. I had gotten away from my true desire, which was and has always been to help others. I had allowed life to take me in a different direction. I wasn't happy, but I just couldn't figure out why. I was making more money, and I was working as a social worker, but my heart just wasn't in the right place. I had become complacent. I was simply going through the motions and focusing more on the paperwork required for my job rather than the people I was there to help. I had allowed myself to be influenced by negative people around me. I wasn't living up to my full, God-given potential.

I wish there could have been a different event, other than my son's suicide, to make me realize that I needed to get my life back on the right path. I would give anything if Brandon were still here with me, helping others understand depression and suicidal thoughts and inspiring others to have hope! That just wasn't God's plan. I don't understand it, but I don't have to. Now the hardest part begins….

I want be childlike in my faith and belief in God. As the Bible says, "But Jesus said, 'Suffer the little children, and forbid them not, to come unto me; for to such belongeth the kingdom of heaven'" (Matthew 19:14). I want to open my eyes with childlike innocence. I want to belong in the kingdom of heaven. It is not enough for me to identify God's plan for my life. I must be open to see what his true vision is for me. Once I am sure of his plan, I must keep worldly beliefs, the devil, and negative people from discouraging me.

I think it is extremely important for us to remember what our hopes and dreams were when we were small children, before life affected us and caused us to doubt ourselves and our ability to make anything we desired happen.

Again, I am going to ask you to utilize the inserted pages and write down who you wanted to be when you were little, in your teens, and at the different stages in your adulthood.

Who I Was and Wanted to Be when I Was a Young Child.

Who I Was and Wanted to Be as a Teenager.

Who I Was and Wanted to Be as a Young Adult.

Cindy Curtis Johnson

Who I Was and Wanted to Be When I Was a Little Girl

I remember thinking that I could accomplish anything I wanted when I younger (actually, this stage only lasted until I was six years old). Until then, I had stayed at home with my mother or played with neighborhood friends and my cousins. I was around adults a lot. My mother and father always talked to me like I was an adult. I remember learning to read before I ever started school. I knew my alphabet, all my colors, and many Bible verses and songs. When I started school, I was so small that all of the children called me the baby. My first grade teacher was wonderful. She knew that hurt me. She also knew how smart I was. She had me teach some of my other classmates how to read. She encouraged me.

Unfortunately, in second grade, I had a teacher who was very critical of my handwriting. Everyone was taught to write with a large pencil back then. Because my hands were so small, it was difficult for me to hold the pencil and write as well as the other children in my classroom did. Up until that point, I had always excelled at everything I tried. I expected myself to be able to accomplish anything. That teacher told my mother that I would never be able to write well because of the size of my hands. Her words caused me to quit trying. To this day, I have the most horrible handwriting. As far as teachers or adults go, she was my first negative influence. I can still remember how sad her words and actions made me. It brings tears to my eyes. I still remember how my spirit was broken because that teacher didn't believe in me.

I have always known that I have a purpose. I have always known I wanted to help people. At a very early age, I started writing plays and would get my neighborhood friends to help me act them out for our parents. The plays were usually about helping people in some way.

I was very sensitive and caring. I never judged people who were "different." I had the philosophy that we are all different because God created us that way. I remember scolding my classmates when they would look and laugh at the children who were in special classes or who looked different than they did.

My best friend at that time was overweight. I remember how angry I got at her mother when she would tell her she was fat and needed to lose weight. I remember researching and writing diet and exercise plans for her to follow. When a new boy moved to town and didn't like my friend, I got angry with him because he didn't like her. I knew it was because of her size. I confronted him and told him that her physical appearance shouldn't matter to him and that she deserved better than him.

I feel incredibly fortunate to have grown up in a Christian home. I always enjoyed attending Sunday school and participating in vacation Bible school. I loved having Bible stories read to me and learning Bible verses. The "golden rule" was one of my favorites: "Therefore, whatever you want men to do to you, do also to them, for this is the Law and the Prophets" (Matthew 7:12). I was so innocent and protected from life's cruelties.

Before entering junior high school, I witnessed to my friends whose parents smoked and drank alcohol. I had always been in a Presbyterian church and believed their teachings that Christians weren't supposed to drink or abuse their bodies in any way because their bodies were created by God. I didn't care if they liked what I had to say or not. At that point in my life, witnessing was far more important than being accepted by my friends.

I remember being told many times, by adults, that I was mature beyond my years. I believe I was born with an old soul. I think the fact that I was an only child and was surrounded by adults so early in life added to my maturity level, but most of all, I believe God created me the way he wanted and needed me to be. Unfortunately, that innocence didn't last long, and I allowed outside forces to influence me and keep me from being the person I was meant to be for far too long.

Who I Was and Wanted to Be as a Teenager

During my early teens, I still was convicted in my beliefs and values. Church was still something I enjoyed. I prayed daily, read my Bible, and continued to find strength in faith. I suppose I was considered a nerd by many, actually; I was told that several years later when I was elected a cheerleader.

I was very shy as a young child and during my early teen years. I had been called a baby, midget, and "shorty." You see, I was always either the shortest child in school or next to the shortest. I looked younger than my peers, and I related better with adults than I did with other children. Since, I was an excellent student, quiet, and eager to learn, I was often the teacher's pet. That made other children like me even less. In my early teen years, I remember crying at night because I didn't want to go to school and have people make fun of me.

I, like most children, went through a very awkward stage. I wore braces, had pimples and bad hair, and still was much smaller than everyone else my age. During that time in my life, I don't really remember thinking about God's plan for me, but I did think of who I wanted to be. I wanted to be popular, be accepted by everyone, and have people want to be like me.

I have always had a big heart, and I continued to care for others even when I went through the stage where God's plan for my life wasn't even a thought. I just wanted worldly adoration more than I wanted what is truly important in life—God's plan.

In eighth grade, I and one of my friends decided we were going to practice and try out for cheerleading. My junior high school was from sixth to ninth grade. The student body elected the cheerleaders, so I didn't even think I had a chance of being chosen as a cheerleader. I wasn't in the popular crowd, and they were the ones who got picked for everything!

Imagine my surprise when my name, along with the names of three of the most popular girls, was called out to come to the principal's office. At first, it didn't even cross my mind that I was being called to the office to find out I was going to be a cheerleader. The other three girls didn't think so either. One of them told me, "I thought it had to be about us being chosen as cheerleaders until I heard your name." You see, the popular girls' votes were split because they all shared the same friends. I later found out that I got the highest number of votes because a lot of the "unpopular" kids voted for me.

Being chosen by my classmates to be on the cheerleading squad was such an honor to me. I will never forget how happy I was when I was first told. Shortly afterward, that happiness turned into sadness because a lot of my previous "unpopular" friends stopped talking to me. They said I had changed because I was part of the popular group. What they didn't realize was that I didn't change. I was still the same person. I didn't understand why they weren't happy for me. I felt certain that if the circumstances had been different and they had been chosen instead of me, I would have been happy for them.

It was amazing to me how I "came to life" as part of a cheerleading squad. As a result of being made fun of for being so short, I had become very self-conscious. As part of a group, I thrived. I wasn't the most coordinated person on the squad. I spent hours practicing the cheers and especially the dances. Most of the girls on the squad had taken dance classes and were part of dance teams. I had never taken any dance lessons.

As I accomplished learning cheers and dance routines, my confidence level increased. I started to believe in myself, as I had done when I was a little girl, before I started school and had other children make fun of me.

In ninth grade, I was again elected as a cheerleader. The squad voted for captain and co-captain, and I, much to my surprise, was chosen as captain. My confidence level soared.

This was around the same time when several of the squad members told me, "Boys don't like you if you are smart." I then decided that I would stop studying and would make Cs because I had to keep a C average to stay on the cheerleading squad.

It's so funny looking back and seeing how easily persuaded I was when I was a teenager. Being popular and especially being liked by boys were far more important than staying true to myself. This was also the time that I starting drinking alcohol and smoking.

When I entered high school, I guess I was considered one of the "popular girls." I never viewed myself that way. I was still that insecure little girl who felt like I was trying to be someone I was not. Looking back, I think that is exactly what I was doing.

In the group setting of my cheerleading squad, I was comfortable. It didn't bother me at all to be in a gymnasium cheering in front of hundreds of people. I didn't have that confidence level when I was alone.

I will never forget how scared I was when I had to present a book report in front of my senior English class. I was terrified. My voice shook, my face turned white, and I thought I was going to faint. I remember my classmates telling me how sorry they felt for me when I was in front of them presenting. They could all tell how scared I was.

Because of my inner shyness and lack of self-confidence at that time in my life, I never wanted a job that would require me to market or sell anything. I drank and experimented with drugs, in large part to try to fit in. When I was under the influence, I didn't feel shy. I wasn't. I was far more confident after a couple of drinks.

Even during my most self-destructive phases in high school, I always knew I wanted to do something in life that would help others. My cheerleading sponsor had such a positive influence on me. She was my psychology/sociology teacher. When she spoke about having her degree in social work, I knew what I wanted to do. I decided that social work would be my major when I entered college.

When I planned to go to Middle Tennessee State University and major in social work, it was a simple choice for me. My uncle and cousins had attended the same college. Murfreesboro wasn't that far from home, and many of my friends from high school were also planning to go there. One of my best friends and I planned to be roommates. It was an exciting but scary time.

My father worked out of town the last few years I was in high school. His company agreed for him to remain in Fayetteville until I graduated; however, after graduation, they expected him to relocate. We had lived in the same home my entire life. Even though I was planning to leave for college after summer was over, it was really difficult moving from the only home I had ever known shortly after high school graduation.

The summer between high school and college was a learning experience for me. My parents and I moved to Columbia, Tennessee. All of a sudden, my close friends were a couple of counties away. The home I had always known was occupied by strangers, and I could no longer walk to my grandparents' house or store. I missed everything, and I was scared of my pending adulthood.

Suddenly, instead of being with all my friends whom I had known since first grade, I was the new girl in town. I got all kinds of new attention, especially from boys. It was exciting but really scary at the same time.

I'll never forget the day I moved into the dorm at MTSU. My friend who was supposed to be my roommate had decided over the summer that she didn't want to leave her grandmother. She had enrolled in beauty school and didn't call to let me know that she had changed her mind about going to college. When my parents dropped me off, after they helped me move into my dorm room, I remember experiencing an overwhelming sadness. I felt all alone and incredibly afraid of what lay ahead for me.

Luckily, within days of moving in the dorm, I realized that some of my friends from high school lived in the same dorm, just on a different floor. Living in the dorm room next to theirs was a girl whose roommate hadn't shown up either. I was able to move into the room with her. After that, I quickly adjusted to dorm life and started to enjoy my college experience.

At the end of my first semester, I was introduced to my first husband by a couple of my high school friends. We started dating at the beginning of my second semester and got married when I was twenty years old.

During my teen years, I knew I wanted to get married and have two children. My plan at that time included working for about ten years and then having children. My dream was to have a boy and a girl. I planned to stay at home with them until they started school and then return to the workforce. Of course, none of this happened in the order I had planned. I have found out in life, especially over the past few years, that I simply am not in control of those things I think I am in control of. Actually, God is in control, and I'm just along for the ride. It's what I choose to do with the circumstances I face that will either make or break me.

Who I Was and Wanted to Be as a Young Adult

As most little girls do, I always dreamed of being a bride one day and having a dream wedding. I remember asking my parents for a wedding dress, veil, and blond wig for Christmas when I was about four years old. My parents still have the picture of me dressed in that outfit on Christmas morning.

When my first husband and I got engaged, we planned a wedding. We scheduled the date, prepared for the wedding, got the dress, had a shower, and then got into a fight and called it off. We made up a few days later and got married at the courthouse. When I got married at twenty years of age, I planned to remain in college and complete my degree. I continued to have the same desires I had when I was younger. Helping others and having a healthy, happy family were still my primary goals.

At twenty-one years of age, much to my first husband's and my surprise, we learned I was pregnant. I was taking birth control pills and obviously either missed one or was on an antibiotic that caused the pill to become ineffective. Krissie, our unexpected little bundle of joy, was born in March of 1987. I am happy to say that I remained in college and graduated with my bachelor of social work degree in May of that same year. Krissie was in the crowd clapping for me as I walked across the stage to get my diploma.

My four-foot-eleven-inch body just wasn't made for carrying babies. With Krissie, I was placed on medication to help stop contractions early in my pregnancy. Despite the medication, I went into full-blown labor seven weeks early. By the time I arrived at Maury Regional Medical Center, I was already dilated to six centimeters. I was rushed to Vanderbilt University Medical Center, where I continued to have contractions daily for three weeks. Every day, I was told she would be born by midnight. I was shown babies in the NICU. People everywhere were praying for me and Krissie. The day before she was born, I had an amniocentesis. I was told that she would weigh three and half pounds at the most if she was born then. The next day, which just happened to be my twenty-second birthday, Krissie was born. She weighed five pounds nine ounces and was a perfectly healthy baby. She was my first miracle baby. There was no medical explanation for her weight and health. I knew all the prayers had been answered and God was the reason for my precious gift.

I was so happy when Krissie was able to go home from the hospital with me two days after her birth. I felt blessed to be able to stay at home with her and not have to work outside the home. Even though my marriage had been extremely rocky during the pregnancy, everything seemed to be going better.

My first husband and I wanted our children to be two years apart in age, so Brandon was a planned pregnancy. I was so excited when I got pregnant the first month after we decided to try for another baby. At three months, I started having contractions. I was put on bed rest for the remainder of my pregnancy with him. It was so difficult. Krissie was used to it just being the two of us at home together during the day. She was a mommy's girl and didn't like going to anyone but me. My mother stayed with us as long as she could, and then a friend started staying there, caring for Krissie during the day so I could stay off my feet.

Despite all the difficulties I experienced during my pregnancy with Brandon, he was born with minimal health problems. On June 15, 1989, Brandon was born. At first, he couldn't breathe on his own and was placed on oxygen. As had been the case with my pregnancy with Krissie, many people were praying for Brandon and me. Within twenty-four hours of his birth, he was breathing on his own and was able to come home with me three days afterward. Again, I felt so blessed.

My life appeared to be heading in the direction I had always dreamed. I was a stay-at-home wife and mother with the little girl and little boy I had always wanted and dreamed of. I remember praising God. My relationship with him grew. I knew that without him, neither of my children would have been born healthy. I was so grateful for all the people who prayed for my children and me during my difficult pregnancies. I knew there was a *great* purpose for my children's and my life.

My first marriage was rocky from the start, but after Brandon's birth, things appeared to be better than ever. Actually, eleven months after his birth, we decided to renew our wedding vows. My first husband was Catholic, so we went through counseling with the priest and renewed our vows on our fifth wedding anniversary.

A couple of months after the renewal of our vows, my ex-husband told me that he didn't want the responsibility of a wife and children. He told me that he loved me but "wasn't in love with me." Suddenly, my world turned upside down.

At twenty-five years of age, with two children, I was on my own. I moved back in with my parents and found a job. My dream of being a stay-at-home wife and mother was over. Once again, life proved to be something of which I was not in control.

I was forced to change my goals and dreams for life. I had to make a living for my children and myself. Instead of staying home with my children while they were small, I was forced by my circumstances to enter the workforce. I was fortunate that I found a social work job. I loved the people I worked for and with. I was making a difference in the lives of others. It just wasn't the timing or situation I had planned.

Literally within days of starting my new job, I met my current husband. I truly believe God put him in my life at the exact time I needed him most. He is twelve years older than me. If we had met before, I wouldn't have even considered entering into a relationship with him. The first night we met, we talked for hours. I tried to scare him away by telling him about every difficulty in my life. It obviously didn't work.

Glenn accepted my children as his own from the very beginning. He was the only father Brandon ever remembered. Krissie was a lot slower warming up to him. She called him "Dr. Johnson" for at least a year. He liked to drink sweet tea when she was little, so she started calling him "Dr. Tea." When she realized he wasn't likely to exit her life, "Dr. Tea" became "Daddy Glenn" and eventually, "Daddy." When Krissie and Brandon were old enough to stand in court and say whom they wanted their father to be, they did so. On that day, Glenn became their "legal" father.

Until Brandon's death, we really hadn't experienced too many difficulties. We had lost several family members, including three of Glenn's aunts, one of his cousins, his father, and my grandmother, granny, ex-mother-in-law, and grandfather. We have lived comfortably; however, the majority of our marriage, I have worked outside the home.

One of my biggest regrets is that I didn't stay at home with the children when they were little. I also regret taking a job in 1996 and 1997 where I travelled a lot. I missed being here for many of Brandon's events.

Somewhere along the way, making money became more important to me than truly helping others. I also didn't put God first, as I had done when I was younger. As a result, I became very unhappy, my health declined, and I wasn't the mother or wife I wish I had been.

Chapter 5

Identifying the Person You Want to Become

For I know the plans I have for you, declares the Lord.
—Jeremiah 29:11

Again, I am going to encourage you to utilize the inserted pages and write down a description of the person you want to become. I am going to do the same in this chapter.

Since Brandon's death, I have become extremely interested in learning as much as I can about suicide. It took me a while to accept that he took his own life. I still don't understand why. I don't think I ever will. I just know that I want to help other people not to make the same decision he made. I also want to help others who have lost someone as a result of suicide by sharing my story and offering support groups. I want to educate the community so everyone has a better understanding of this subject.

Identifying the Person You Want to Become.

Identifying the Person You Want to Become.

Identifying the Person You Want to Become.

Identifying the Person You Want to Become.

Identifying the Person You Want to Become.

Shortly after Brandon's death, his fraternity brothers held a benefit in his memory. Glenn, Krissie, Daniel, Noah, and I attended this event. A representative from the Tennessee Suicide Prevention Network (TSPN) was there. He had a table set up which included information about suicide and about support groups and resources for survivors. There was also a quilt display which contained pictures of persons who had completed suicide in Tennessee. My husband and I were immediately drawn to this display and the representative. We spoke with the gentleman at the table and shared our story.

I couldn't help but notice how all the college students, including Krissie and Daniel, avoided the TSPN table and the volunteer. They wouldn't even look at the quilt or information. You could immediately see how uncomfortable they were with the topic. I found it ironic that the event was to honor Brandon's memory, yet the topic of suicide was something no one wanted to discuss or remember. Don't get me wrong; I want my son remembered for the way he lived, not the way he died. However, this event was to raise money for a not-for-profit organization that his fraternity had adopted for their philanthropy after his death. It was specifically chosen because it dealt with depression and suicidal ideation. Yet no one wanted to discuss that.

I mentioned earlier how uncomfortable I was speaking in front of people. This really hadn't changed a lot in my adult years. It is amazing to me how much Brandon's death has changed me. Not only do I feel like a different person inside, but I am a different person outside as well. I was always so worried about other people's opinions and perceptions of me. Now I'm not. I believe one of the reasons for my lack of self-confidence prior to Brandon's death was because I feared rejection from others.

Now that I have experienced the most terrible thing I could have ever imagined, I no longer fear rejection. Brandon's suicide taught me that people are going to judge regardless of whether they know you or not. Hours after Brandon's suicide, we were hearing stories about things other people were saying about him. People who didn't even know my son were saying things like "He slit his wrist" and "He was always troubled." These comments were hurtful to our family, particularly because they simply weren't true. One good outcome of this is that I realized for the first time in my life that some people judge and voice their opinions no matter what you do. It was as if a lightbulb went off in my head. I immediately stopped caring about what other people thought and decided that I was going to live my life for God. I started thinking of how I could make a substantial difference in the lives of others. I now realize that life is just too short to worry about other people's opinions.

Since I have become involved as a volunteer with TSPN, I have spoken at a number of events. The first time I was asked to "share my story" at a TSPN event, I was apprehensive. I prayed all night before and up until the moment I stood in front of the eighty people in attendance. I prayed that God would give me the strength and the words to reach that crowd. He did just that. I had confidence and strength that I never imagined. After I finished sharing my story, numerous people came up to me and thanked me for sharing. Many of them opened up and shared stories of their own losses due to suicide. Some even shared their own struggles with depression and suicidal thoughts. I was encouraged by their comments and openness. Several of them encouraged me to continue speaking. I remember one person in particular who had lost a child several years before. She said, "Please tell me you are going to continue sharing your story. You will be able to help so many people if you do." Her words not only encouraged but inspired me to continue speaking.

The second time I spoke with TSPN, it was to a group of professors at an art institute. They had specifically requested that TSPN come and do a "postvention training" for them. They had lost three students to suicide in a five-year period. This time, I was able to tell the professors how I felt as a parent when the school didn't even act as if they cared about my son's death. Again, my words were well received and touched them in ways I hadn't even expected. Several of them came up to me afterwards and said they now knew they had "incorrectly handled situations with parents." One professor even said that she was going to call the family after hearing my story. I helped inspire them to speak with their administration about putting a postvention plan in place.

The third time I spoke was at the TSPN tenth anniversary symposium. There were approximately 220 people in attendance. I was on the survivors' panel. Again, I prayed for the strength and words to reach others. God, again, granted that to me. My story was well received. I was told afterwards that I was an inspiration. People always comment that they don't know how I have the strength and courage to speak about my son's suicide so soon after his death. I continue to explain that it is God's strength and not mine that allows me to do this.

In addition to the events above, I have also shared my story several times with college students and senior care providers. I serve on the older person committee with TSPN. We have a suicide prevention presentation that we use to educate persons who provide care to the senior population. I have also completed training to be a QPR trainer. QPR stands for Question, Persuade, and Refer. It is a leading suicide prevention program. With TSPN's assistance, I have started a Survivors of Suicide support group in Clarksville. My work and church have supported this effort and helped make it a reality. Local media outlets have also been very helpful. They have allowed me to record PSAs, podcasts, and advertisements for the support group. Channel 4 News even did a story about our group and included it on the ten o'clock news.

I have attended a seminar on how to set up a nonprofit foundation. I initially wanted to set up a foundation so I could provide more suicide awareness, prevention, and postvention services. I may still do this; however, I want to make sure it is God's will before I pursue it further.

In helping others, I don't want to lose sight of the needs of my family. When Brandon first died, he was all I could think about. I had a new grandson, Noah, who was the light of my life. He was born in March before Brandon's death in September. I was so caught up in my grief that I distanced myself from Noah, and everyone else, for a while. I regret that but realize it was my way of coping at the time.

The person I now want to become is the best mother, grandmother, wife, daughter, friend, and inspirational writer and speaker I can be. I now realize that if I allow God to direct my path, I can accomplish *anything!* I believe God wanted me to write this book and wants me to go out and speak to others. I believe that within the year, I will be speaking all over the county in a tour titled "The Hope from Tragedy Tour."

> **You will succeed in all you do, and**
> **light will shine on your path.**
> **—Job 22:28**

CHAPTER 6

Forgiving and Letting Go of Past Hurts

For if ye forgive men their trespasses, our heavenly Father will also forgive you. But if ye forgive not men their trespasses, neither will your Father forgive your trespasses.
—**Matthew 6:14-15**

As I write this chapter, I am sitting in a hotel room in Anniston, Alabama. My mother-in-law celebrated her ninetieth birthday on July 13, 2011. My husband and sister-in-law planned a party for today, Saturday, July 16. It is now 10:35 AM. The party begins at 2:00 PM.

I originally did not plan to attend this party. You see, my mother-in-law and I have *never* been close. Actually, I always win the worst mother-in-law story when I tell about our first meeting. I met her twenty-one years ago. You have to understand the way my husband described his mother to me on the long ride to Memphis, Tennessee. He told me that his mother was the kindest, most loving person he had ever known. I was truly expecting to meet a little lady who would hug, kiss, and thank me for making her son so happy. Quite the opposite occurred. The very first thing she did was take me into her living room. Glenn and his father stayed in the kitchen talking. She immediately pulled out a picture of one of my husband's ex-girlfriends, showed it to me, and said, "This is the one we wanted him to marry, but he didn't love her like he does you, Hun!" At twenty-five years of age, with two children from a previous marriage and just coming out of an abusive marriage, I was crushed by her words. I didn't even know how to respond. As you know from reading earlier chapters in this book, my ex-mother-in-law and I were extremely close. We were close from the first time we met. I just wasn't equipped to handle not being someone's "first choice" for her son.

Over the past twenty-one years, I have attempted to get my mother-in-law to like me. I know in my heart that I have tried as hard as I possibly could have. Despite her never remembering my birthday, I actually planned her eightieth birthday party. I made a collage of pictures, made the invitations on my home computer, compiled the guest list, mailed the invitations, decorated for the party, and played hostess. The only thing she really said to me, in private, was that there were people left off the guest list who should have been on it. I have always bought her very expensive outfits for every occasion and even offered to quit my job and stay home and care for her in our home when she got to the point where it was unsafe for her to live alone. Her response to my husband was "Do you think Cindy would mistreat me?" All of my attempts to win her over have been to no avail. The only thing that is different now is that she has dementia and I don't think she remembers how much she truly dislikes me.

For years, she called me by the ex-girlfriend's name. When Glenn's father died, the ex-girlfriend showed up at the funeral and sat with the family. When my sister-in-law finally confronted my mother-in-law about calling me by the ex's name, she attempted to apologize to me and actually made it even worse. She said, "I don't mean to call you by that name. It's just that she and I still talk on the phone a lot, and we're very close."

When Brandon died, I didn't hear from her at all. Everyone kept making excuses for her, saying that her memory was terrible, but I knew she was talking to Glenn every day about it. After many days had gone by, Glenn was on the phone with her and she asked to speak to me. He and I both were excited because we thought she was going to ask how I was holding up and tell me that she was thinking of me. As soon as I answered the phone, her words to me were, "Cindy, I'm so worried about Glenn since Brandon died." I immediately threw the cell phone across the room and burst into tears. It was bad enough that I hadn't heard from her at all since Brandon's suicide; the fact that she didn't even ask how I was the first time she did speak to me made it even worse.

I'm crying while writing this. I am still so hurt by it all. I hate the feelings I am experiencing today. I forced myself to come here in an attempt to forgive and forget. I am really struggling. Yesterday, when we arrived, I saw her for the first time since well before Brandon's death. She smiled at me and said she was glad I was here. I think she really meant it, but I'm not even sure she really knows who I am.

I have all these feelings that I know I shouldn't have. I am so angry that she has lived to be ninety years old and still has both of her children. I'm angry that my husband thinks his mother is so sweet despite the fact that she has treated me horribly for the past twenty-one years. I'm upset that he expects me to forgive her and let go of all the hurt and pain she has caused. I'm angry that he and his sister are throwing her yet another "once-in-a-lifetime birthday party." Her eightieth birthday party was supposed to have been that. She asked for it because she didn't think she would live to be ninety. When she lived to be eighty-five, she asked for a party then as well. Now she has had three "once-in-a-lifetime parties." Today, over eighty people have been invited to attend. I'll hear all afternoon what a sweet mother-in-law I have and be told how lucky I am to be her daughter-in-law. How is it possible that everyone else knows such a different person than I do? Why can't I see that sweet little old lady everyone else seems to see?

I am here to let go of this ... I just have to move past it. I have to accept the fact that she will never like me and I will never like her. I have to forgive her. I have to attempt to forget what she has said and done in the past so I can move forward. I just want this hurt to go away. I can't believe I am crying over this.

I've spoken with a lot of people lately about their experiences with family and friends after the suicides of their loved ones. There is one central theme that seems to exist, and that is that each survivor feels like they now know whom their true friends are. I don't know why I thought my mother-in-law would be there in some small way for me when Brandon died. She never was before. I was surprised and shocked by who really was there in the beginning and who wasn't. I'm even more shocked and surprised by the people who haven't remained there.

This past year has been even harder than the first. I have so longed for my friends and family. I don't understand why some of them were there for me during the first few days, weeks, and months and then distanced themselves from me. I don't understand why I still haven't heard anything from some of the people I thought would be there. I just know I have to let go of the pain I feel toward them, as well.

Last night, my sister-in-law, her son, and two of my husband's cousins came to our hotel room and visited with us. It didn't really shock me that two of them who didn't attend the funeral didn't even mention Brandon's death. I would have loved to have them acknowledge his loss, but I understand people just simply don't know what to say. It also didn't really surprise me that when I was showing pictures of our pool and grandson, including a picture of Brandon holding Noah, everyone ignored that picture and obviously felt very uncomfortable when I mentioned Brandon's name. I just hate that people assume I don't want his name mentioned. I wish they would understand that I want to hear people talk about him. I want them to remember him. I don't want him to be forgotten because he is dead! Why don't they understand that I think about him all the time? People mentioning him or his name isn't going to make me remember his death; it is going to make me know that they, like me, still think of, remember, and miss him.

I know I have to move past the hurt. I have to forgive others for not being there for me in the way I needed them to be. I have to take some responsibility for this. I realize I haven't been the most approachable person since Brandon's death. I'm sure I've even pushed others away or led them to believe I don't need them by appearing so strong on the outside.

I know this is a process. I'm sure I won't be able to forget and completely forgive those people who hurt me by not calling or visiting since Brandon's funeral as quickly as I would like. I just pray that God will grant me the ability to forgive and forget, just as he has granted me the strength to endure Brandon's death.

Forgiving and Letting Go of Past Hurts...

Cindy with her mother-in-law, sister-in-law and husband at her mother-in-law's 90th Birthday Party.

Chapter 7

Hope for a Bright and Productive Future

In everything God works for the good of those who love him.
*—**Romans 8:28***

Webster Dictionary defines *hope* as "to cherish or desire with anticipation; to desire with expectation of obtainment; to expect with confidence: trust."

I have known people who literally went to bed after the death of a loved one and willed themselves to die. I have also known people who, years after the death of a loved one, can speak of nothing else. I refuse to allow my life to stop as a result of Brandon's death! I also refuse to give up hope for a bright and productive future!

I encourage you to utilize the note pages inserted in this section and write down everything for which you are grateful. Of course, I am going to do the same below.

Things for Which You Are Grateful

Things for Which You Are Grateful

Things for Which I Am Grateful

- God
- my husband
- my parents
- my children
- my grandchild
- my pets
- my material belongings
- my church
- my friends
- my extended family
- my job
- my health
- my country
- my freedom
- my faith
- life's lessons

This list is by no means everything for which I am grateful. That list could truly go on and on for page after page. My desire for you is that you continue to count your blessings more than dwelling on your difficulties. The list of things for which you are grateful should continue to grow each day of your life.

Dwelling on difficulties and tragedies could consume us if we allow it. I hope you, like me, choose a different path. This life is so short. It would be a shame to miss it because you can't move past a tragic event.

We certainly have to allow ourselves to experience grief, but we don't have to let it consume us. It is important to work through the stages. It is also important that we identify who we want to become.

I know I want to be a person who truly makes a positive difference in the lives of everyone who knows me or comes into contact with me. I don't want to be remembered as that poor mother whose son completed suicide! I want to be remembered as a person who turned the most tragic event in her life into hope for herself and others.

I want my grandson to know me as a happy person, not a grieving person. I want my daughter to know that she is just as important to me as her brother. I don't want her to feel that I focus so much on his death that I forget to concentrate on her life.

Life can be incredibly difficult at times. It can also be very rewarding. I know I will miss my son every day of my life, but I also know how incredibly lucky I was to have had him in my life for twenty years.

I am excited about my future. I know that I will someday be reunited with Brandon in heaven. Until that day, I will remain hopeful for myself and my family's future.

I believe we can make a conscious decision to be hopeful despite difficulties and tragedies in our lives. I know God, not me, is in control. I also know I can decide how I react to the negative and positive events in my life.

I want to continue to educate others regarding suicide prevention, but that is simply no longer enough for me. In addition to that, I want to inspire anyone who has suffered a tragedy to redirect his or her pain into hope for a bright and productive future.

I will make a positive difference. I will be the best person I can possibly be. I will allow God to direct my path. I will follow that path. It is my sincere desire that you will do the same.

I can do all things through Christ which strengtheneth me.
—Philippians 4:13

Blessings Prior to Brandon's Death...

Brandon with Cindy & Glenn at his High School graduation in May of 2007

Brandon with his new nephew, Noah, on March 24, 2009

Brandon with Cindy, Krissie & Noah on Easter Sunday 2009

Brandon with Glenn, Krissie and Noah on Easter Sunday 2009

Continued Blessings Since Brandon's Death…

Glenn, Cindy, Krissie & Noah 2010

Daniel, Krissie & Noah 2011

Cindy & Noah Summer 2011

Becoming the Person I Never Imagined I Could Be...

Cindy with Scott Ridgeway, Executive Director of TSPN and
Clarksville City Mayor Kim McMillan 2011
image: Courtesy of www.clarksvillenow.com

Cindy with Montgomery County Mayor, Carolyn Bowers 2011
image: Courtesy of www.clarksvillenow.com

Cindy on the Survivors of Suicide Panel at the TSPN
10th Anniversary Symposium in 2011.

CPSIA information can be obtained at www.ICGtesting.com
Printed in the USA
LVOW062022231211

260936LV00001B/7/P

9 781462 712076